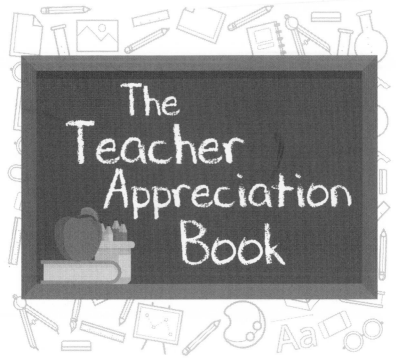

# The Teacher Appreciation Book

This Book of Appreciation
Is For The One, The ONLY,

_____!

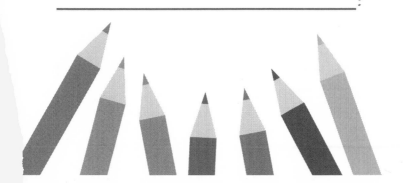

# Teacher

(n.) One who inspires, guides, enlightens, motivates; tireless scholar.

_____,
thank you for being
my teacher!

A good teacher, like a good entertainer, first must hold their audience's attention, then they can teach their lesson.

-John Henrik Clarke

Top 3 reasons you're
the BEST teacher:

1._____

2._____

3._____

Education breeds confidence. Confidence breeds hope. Hope breeds peace.

-Confucius

My favorite subject
to learn with you is

_____.

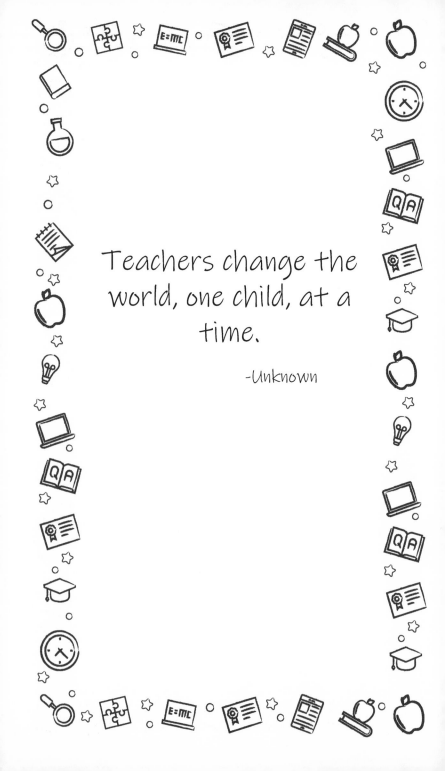

Teachers change the world, one child, at a time.

-Unknown

What I am going to miss most is

_____

_____ .

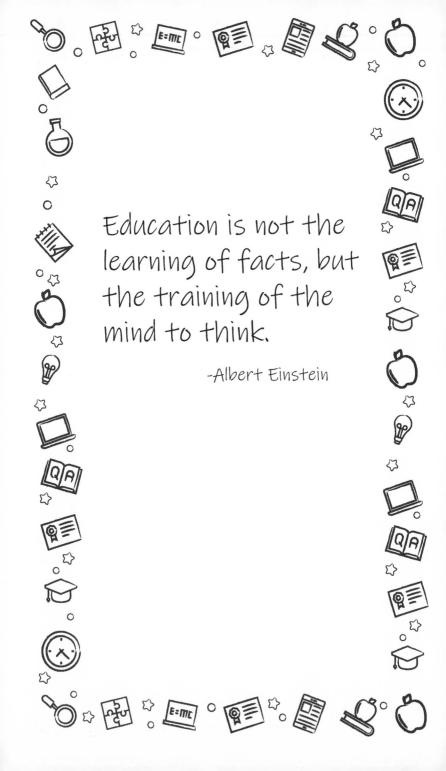

Education is not the learning of facts, but the training of the mind to think.

-Albert Einstein

My teacher always
loves when my class

_____

_____ `

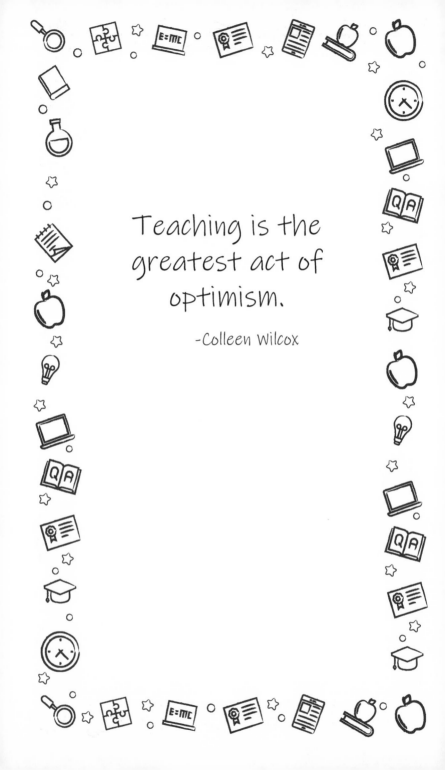

Teaching is the
greatest act of
optimism.

-Colleen Wilcox

One day I hope to

_____
_____
_____!

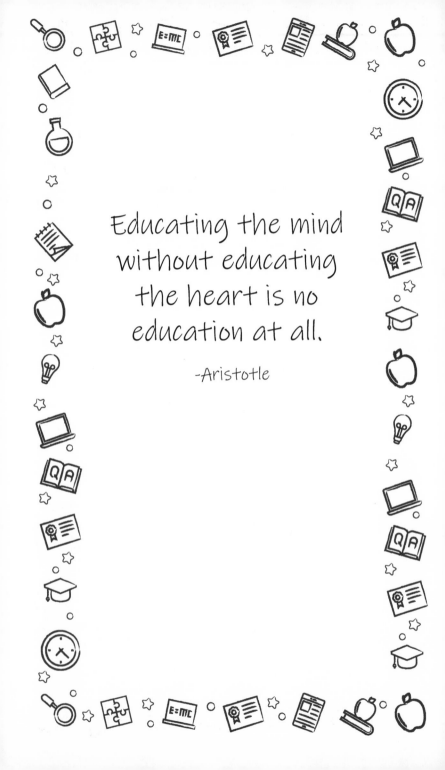

Educating the mind without educating the heart is no education at all.

-Aristotle

I am so _____
to be able to call you
my Teacher.

The best thing about being a teacher is that it matters.

The hardest thing about being a teacher is that it matters every day.

-Todd Whitaker

You make my day
brighter every time you
_____
in class.

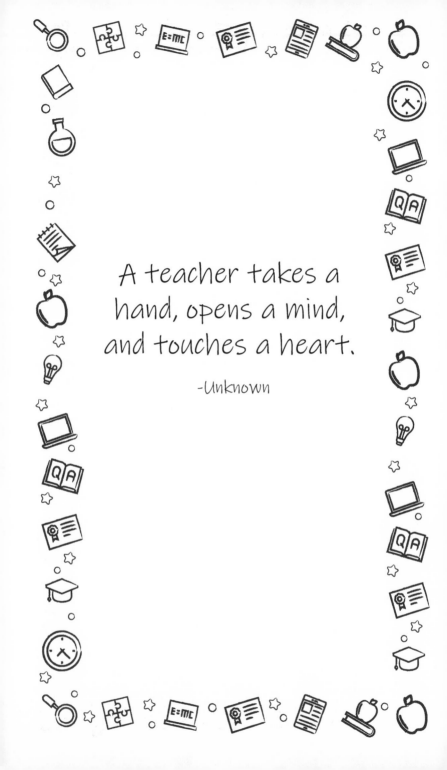

A teacher takes a hand, opens a mind, and touches a heart.

-Unknown

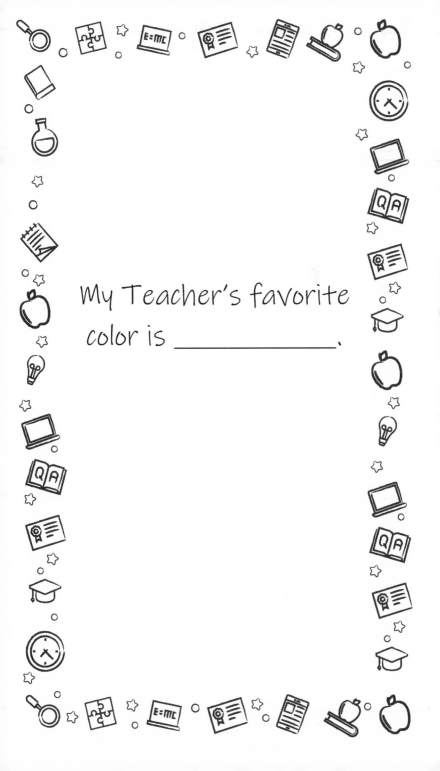

My Teacher's favorite color is _____.

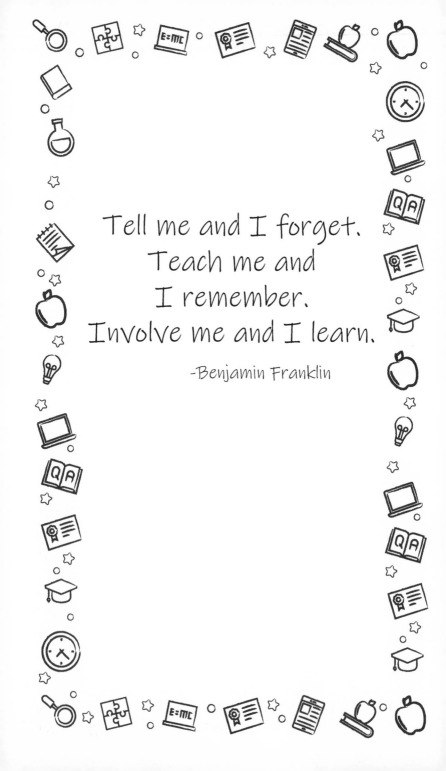

Tell me and I forget.
Teach me and
I remember.
Involve me and I learn.

-Benjamin Franklin

You always make me
laugh when you
_____!

People who say it cannot be done should not interrupt those who are doing it.

-George Bernard Shaw

If you weren't a teacher, I think you would make a great

_____.

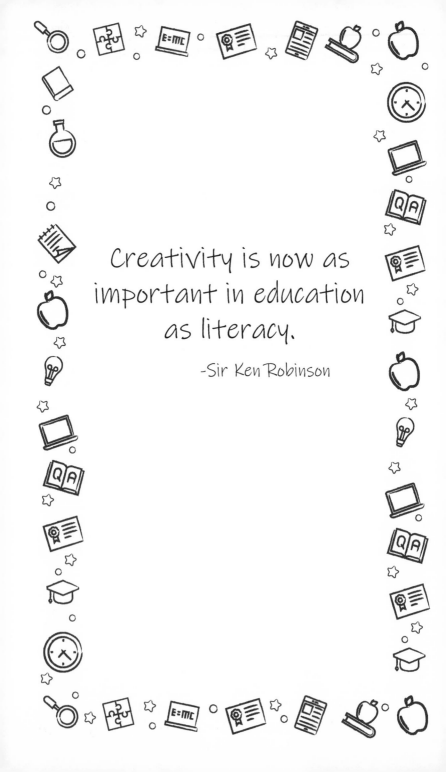

Creativity is now as important in education as literacy.

-Sir Ken Robinson

Nobody can

_____

quite like you!

Children are not
things to be molded,
but people to be
unfolded.

-Jess Lair

I love it when you

_____

_____!

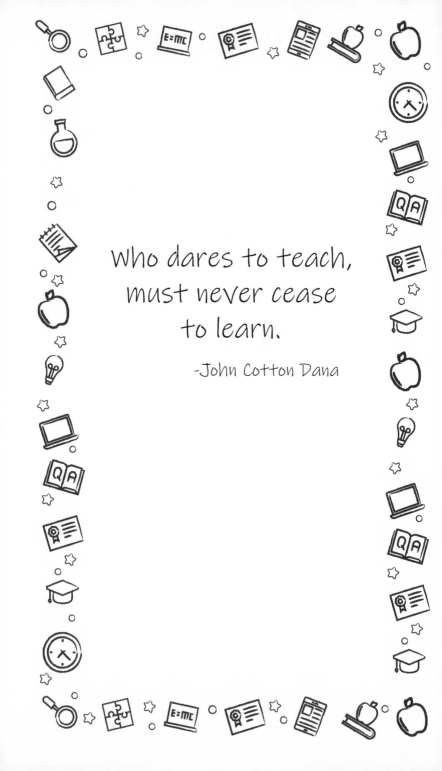

who dares to teach,
must never cease
to learn.

-John Cotton Dana

My Teacher is always
telling me

_____

_____ `

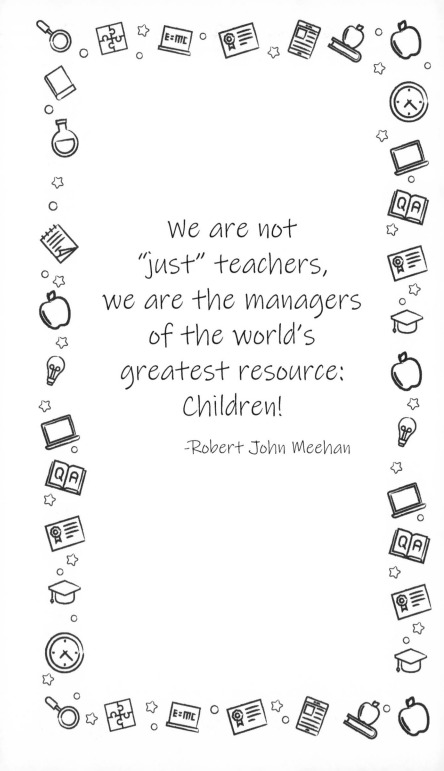

We are not
"just" teachers,
we are the managers
of the world's
greatest resource:
Children!

-Robert John Meehan

I will always
remember

_____

_____ `

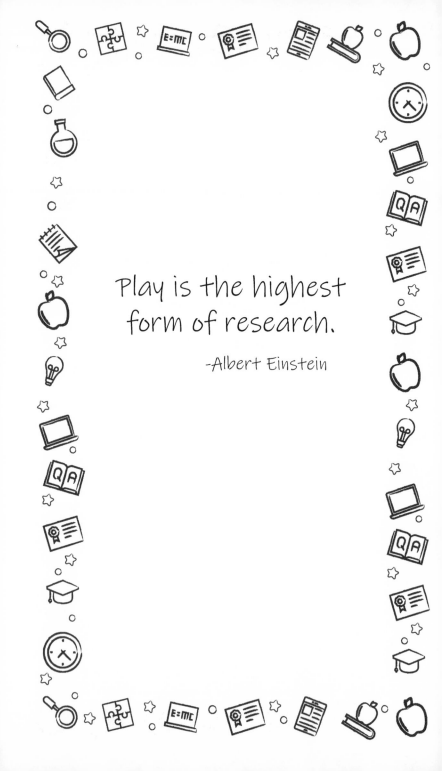

Play is the highest
form of research.

-Albert Einstein

Top 3 words to describe my Teacher are

1. _____

2. _____

3. _____

All kids need is a little help, a little hope, and somebody who believes in them.

-Magic Johnson

My favorite thing I have learned from you this year is

_____

_____.

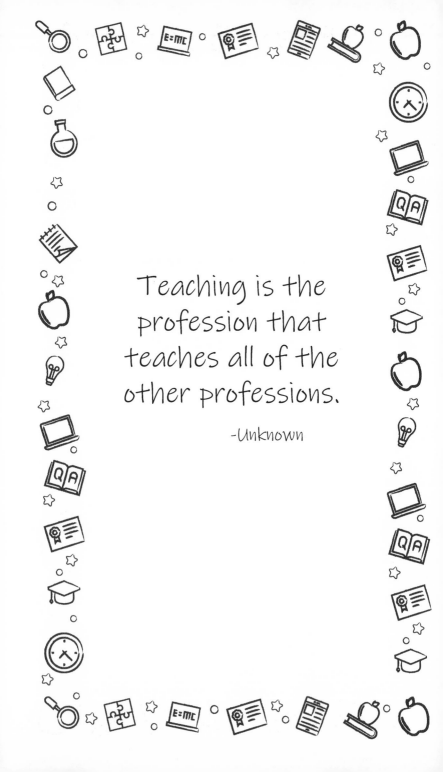

Teaching is the
profession that
teaches all of the
other professions.

-Unknown

Something I did not
expect to learn this
year was

_____

_____.

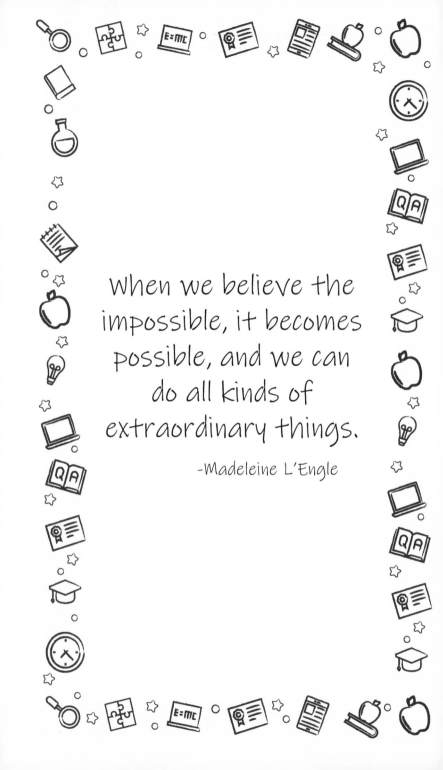

When we believe the impossible, it becomes possible, and we can do all kinds of extraordinary things.

-Madeleine L'Engle

The best thing about
you is

_____
_____!

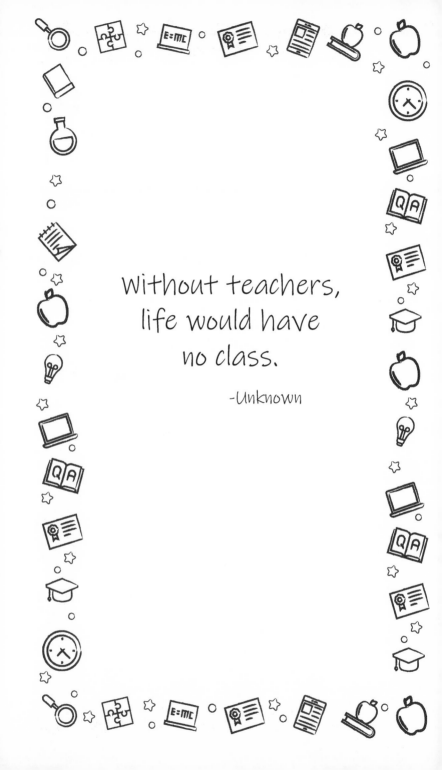

Without teachers,
life would have
no class.

-Unknown

If you had a
superpower, it would
definitely be

_____

_____.

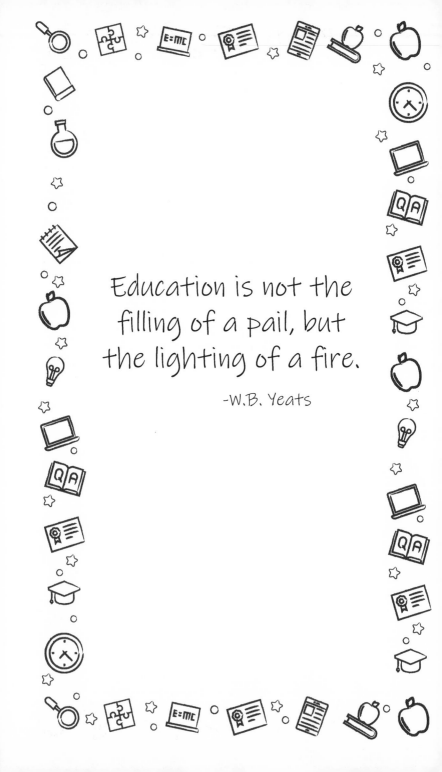

Education is not the filling of a pail, but the lighting of a fire.

-W.B. Yeats

You make me feel

_____

in class.

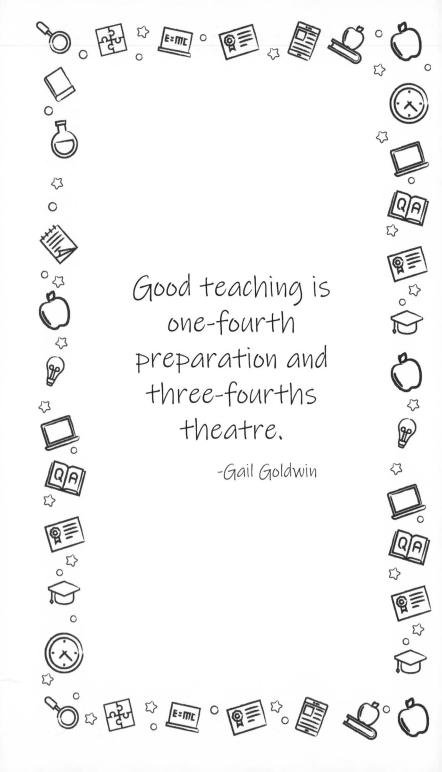

Good teaching is one-fourth preparation and three-fourths theatre.

-Gail Goldwin

You are the

_____

and

_____

teacher EVER!

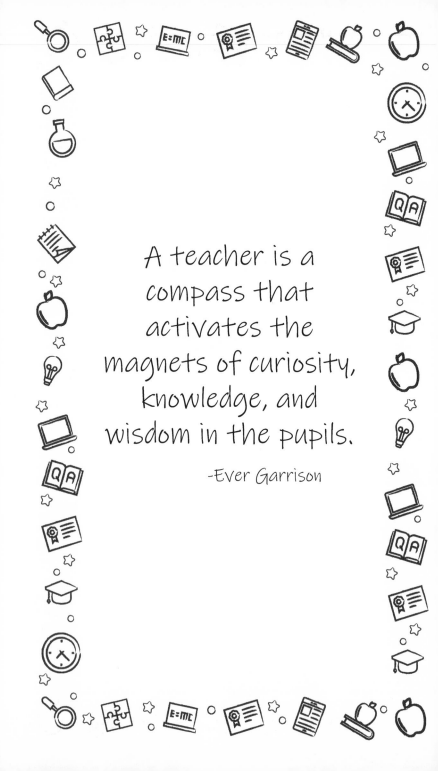

A teacher is a compass that activates the magnets of curiosity, knowledge, and wisdom in the pupils.

-Ever Garrison

I will miss

_____

about our class the
most.

To plant a garden
is to believe
in tomorrow.

-Audrey Hepburn

One last thing I
want to say is

_____

_____

_____!

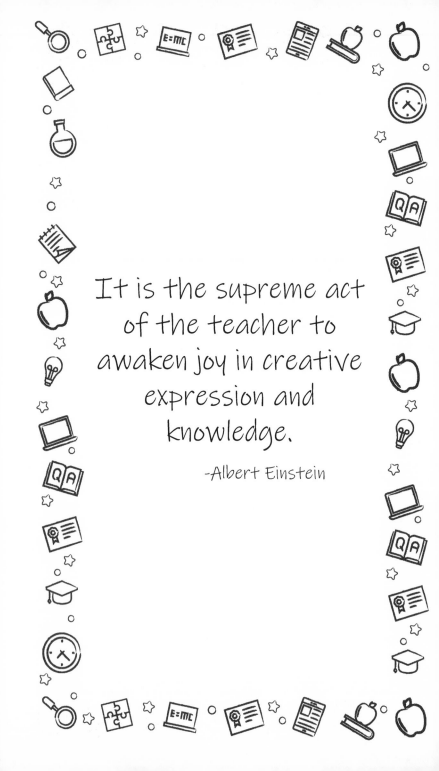

It is the supreme act
of the teacher to
awaken joy in creative
expression and
knowledge.

-Albert Einstein

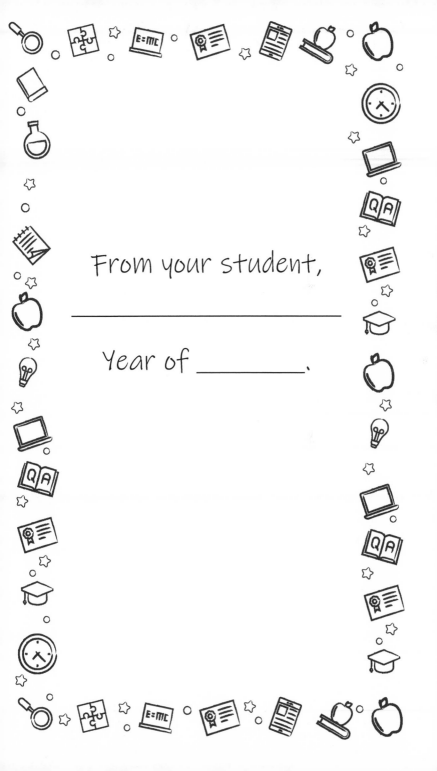

From your student,

_____

Year of _____.

Made in the USA
Monee, IL
16 May 2021